Palace on the Rive

Marcus Binney

Palace on the River

Terry Farrell's redevelopment of Charing Cross

Wordsearch Publishing

First published in Great Britain
in 1991 by
Wordsearch Publishing Ltd
26 Cramer Street
London W1M 3HE
Telephone 071 486 7419

Copyright © 1991 Wordsearch

ISBN 0 951 8284 1X

Design Gabriella Le Grazie
Editing Michael Holmes Coats
*Coordination at Terry Farrell &
Company* Julian Tollast

Printed and bound in
Great Britain by
Balding & Mansell plc
Colour reproduction
Precise Litho Ltd
Text paper
Britannia Silk 150gsm supplied by
Wm. Guppy & Son Ltd

Photography: Cover, 2-3 Nigel Young,
6 Tim Motion, 10-11 Richard Bryant/
Arcaid, 12 from F Dewitt *History of
London,* 14 Alan Williams, 15 Tim
Motion, 17 Jo Reid and John Peck, 18-
19 Alan Williams, 24 National
Monument Records, 26 Ove Arup &
Partners, Northern Photographic
Services, 25 Julian Tollast, 27, 29, 30-
31 Dennis Gilbert, 36 from Payne's
Illustrated London and *London News*
22/6/1867, 39 Nigel Young, 40 Paul
Revere, Richard Cheatle, Grant Smith,
42 Richard Cheatle, Dennis Gilbert,
43 Richard Cheatle, 44 Richard
Cheatle, Dennis Gilbert, Nigel Young,
45 Julian Tollast, 46-47 Alan Williams,
49 Tim Motion, 50 Sarah Nightingale,
52 Nigel Young, Peter Cook, 53 Alan
Williams, 54 John E Linden, 55 Nigel
Young, 56-57 John E Linden, 58 Dennis
Gilbert, 59 Dennis Gilbert, 60 Alan
Williams, 61 Dennis Gilbert, 63, 64, 65
Alan Williams, 66 Nigel Young, 67, 68-
69 Alan Williams, 71 Nigel Young,
Dennis Gilbert, 72 Dennis Gilbert,
Nigel Young, 73 Dennis Gilbert,
74 Nigel Young, 75 Richard Cheatle,
76-77 Alan Williams, 78 Nigel Young,
79, 81 Alan Williams, 94, 96 Nigel
Young.

Contents

Foreword

'The mystification about "architecture" has isolated the intimate building art from the common interest and understanding of ordinary men'. W.R.Lethaby's words are as relevant now as they were in his day, except that there are architects today, like Terry Farrell, who have succeeded in making buildings which are understood, perhaps even loved, by ordinary men. Such a building is Embankment Place, its bold and simple forms by the side of the river – great vaults buttressed by towers – providing instant and irresistible appeal. To court popularity further the building is published here, not critically as in a learned architectural journal, but as hero of a story. Its conception and construction become a great adventure, its description an occasion for admiration and wonder. The language is not the jargon of critics but plain English which may easily be understood by ordinary men.

Embankment Place is a very large building which is designed with great confidence and which never for one moment hesitates to take its place in a family of riverside buildings that includes the Palace of Westminster and Somerset House, as well as the Ministry of Defence and Shell Mex House. Both its central position in the bend of the river and its position on the axis of Hungerford Bridge, give it a focal role so that the eye, observing the panorama from the opposite side of the river, moves involuntarily from the left and right inwards on to the building, which dominates by its sheer size and scale. The building could so easily have been too large, given the economic pressures on this type of development. It was clever of both client and architect to resist the temptation.

Yet if Embankment Place is a very large building, it is also very much more than a building. Terry Farrell's ability to see beyond the building to the urban context was matched by Greycoat's wish to improve the whole area around the building. That it is now possible to walk along Hungerford Bridge into Charing Cross Station or through to the Strand may well be taken for granted, but it must also add considerably to the ordinary person's perception of the building as convenient and functionally successful. That Villiers Street and the passages under Hungerford Bridge and Charing Cross Station are no longer slums, that people can now walk safely from Embankment Underground Station to the Strand without the threat from motor vehicles using the street as a shortcut, that Embankment Gardens have been given a new bandstand, that railings have been put back around the forecourt of Charing Cross Station – that, in short, the whole of the urban landscape around and well beyond the building has been improved almost beyond recognition, must add immeasurably to the ordinary man's perception of the city as an efficient and beautiful place.

Good architecture is the result of creative collaboration between client and architect. The developer as client has tended to put architecture and urban design low on his list of priorities. It has even been said that it is difficult, if not impossible, to make speculative office buildings into architecture, yet the Georgian terrace and square, of which so much of London consists, was speculative development. As a developer, Greycoat has proved to be the exception three times over, with No.1 Finsbury Avenue, Victoria Plaza (both designed by Arup Associates) and now Embankment Place. It has shown that it is not only a good patron of architecture by its choice of architect, but that there is no reason why a commercial office building should not also be a fine piece of architecture.

Sherban Cantacuzino
Royal Fine Arts Commission, November 1991

A new landmark

THAMESIS

FLU.

SOUTH

WEST MUNSTER

BRANDENT LONDON

Left: London in
1666. The pattern
established by the
great houses of
the Strand still
underpins the
form of modern
London.

London has a magnificent new landmark crowning one of the best
of all views over the River Thames. Whether you stand on
Westminster Bridge or Waterloo Bridge the silhouette of Terry
Farrell's building above Charing Cross station forms a new climax
to the whole riverfront from the Houses of Parliament to Somerset
House.

The view is exhilarating precisely because this stretch of the
Thames is so wide, the north side scoured continuously over the
centuries by the weight of the descending current and the
incoming tide.

It was the width of the River, combined with the sharpness of
the bend that begins below Charing Cross – virtually a right angle –
that attracted the view painters. The more distant buildings are
seen not in disappearing perspective but virtually head-on.

This stretch of the River still bears the marks of its long
domination by king and court. Here on the left of Westminster
Bridge stood Whitehall Palace, consumed by fire in the 1690s and
never rebuilt because William III could not abide the damp river air.
Canaletto painted his famous view from the Duke of Richmond's
house beside Westminster Bridge. Beyond stood the houses of
the Duke of Montagu, the Duke of Portland and the Earl of
Pembroke.

On the higher level of the Strand had stood a series of medieval
and Renaissance palaces, both aristocratic and episcopal – York
House, Arundel House, Salisbury House and the Palace of the
Savoy, where John of Gaunt resided.

All these have long vanished, but what survives are the large plot sizes, in utter contrast to the much narrower frontages on the north side of the Strand. So today, as you stand on Westminster Bridge, you see a procession of large imposing buildings with all the monumentality of great public edifices.

The best time to go is on one of those bright, clear, sunny mornings when London is at its most invigorating. At about half-past eight or nine the sun strikes low from the east and the entire curve of the north bank is in brilliant sunshine, presenting a phalanx of gleaming Portland stone façades as white as sugar lumps.

The range begins with the large Government offices punctuated by a row of pedimented roof pavilions, designed by Vincent Harris in 1913, but not completed till much later. Pevsner found it hard to say a good word for them, and they have long been lambasted as the last insipid gasp of classicism, but from a distance, with their brilliant copper roofs, they set the scale for the parade that follows. Next comes the romantic silhouette of Whitehall Court, almost as rich as Chambord.

Then Hungerford Bridge and Farrell's site above the station. Beyond lies Collcutt and Hamp's Adelphi, built from 1936-38 on the site of Robert Adam's masterpiece. Today it can be appreciated as Art Deco at its best, with the sculptural quality and urbanity of the Rockefeller Center. Next door is Joseph's Shell Mex House, dating from 1931, thirteen storeys high with the simple massing of a Thirties mantelpiece clock. Beyond, just as the buildings become more watery in the distance, the Edwardian front of the Savoy Hotel catches the eye with its glistening white tiles.

The Portland stone cliff is completed by the long front of Sir William Chambers' Somerset House, in its length and severe grandeur recalling the Roman Emperor Diocletian's great waterfront palace at Split in Yugoslavia. Just before comes another powerful outcrop of white stone: Brettenham House (1930-32) by W. E. Hunt, on the approach to Waterloo Bridge. What is unusual here is that the rear face of the upper floors, unseen from the street below, is clad in Portland stone precisely to compliment the view from the Embankment and Westminster Bridge.

On the South Bank, County Hall and the Shell Centre are two

Right: Land use, topography and ownership have all contributed to the importance of the site as a 'hinge' between the government and royal areas of Westminster and the commercial zone of the City.

Above: Although the buildings were largely redeveloped between the wars, the size of the riverside sites reflect their origins as aristocratic palaces on this accessible side of the Thames. The use of Portland stone cladding reflects a long tradition of the use of this material for London buildings.

more major monuments clad in blond stonework.

It is, of course, Portland stone that gives much of London, and especially Westminster, its character. It became *de rigueur* because the Crown Commissioners had become exasperated with constantly repainting Nash's stucco (the problem was the smut brought by the railways more than the stucco itself) and insisted that all new buildings on their estate should be clad in stone. All London followed suit.

Portland stone has unusual properties: where it is exposed to wind and rain it remains a constant pristine white. Where it is sheltered it quickly accumulates grime, giving classical buildings a chiaroscuro even on a dull day. On this reach of the River the great Portland stone palaces are constantly lashed by wind and rain, forming a London echo of the white cliffs of Dover.

It was here that Terry Farrell had the opportunity to build. What matched him particularly for the task was his keen eye for Twenties and Thirties architecture, leading him to recognize qualities and draw resonances from neighbouring buildings in a way no other architect working in London would have done.

The new offices had to be distinct enough to hold its own among powerful neighbours, and large enough to support the huge costs of building over a railway terminus in constant use.

Yet nowhere do feelings about bulky new buildings run higher than on the Thames. Geoffrey Wilson, Chairman of Farrell's clients Greycoat, personally selected Farrell among the rising stars in British architecture because he possessed the two qualities most essential for this site – a sense of context and a sense of scale.

Terry Farrell is an architect who positively enjoys working with large masses. So much of twentieth century architecture has concentrated on the character of spaces rather than the walls and roofs that enclose them. The desire for lightness and openness has meant that the tallest buildings are often intended to appear the most ethereal or insubstantial.

Farrell is a master of spatial planning, whether of outdoor urban space, or intriguing sequences of rooms, but it is his ability to make mass and weight a positive virtue that singles him out from virtually all his contemporaries.

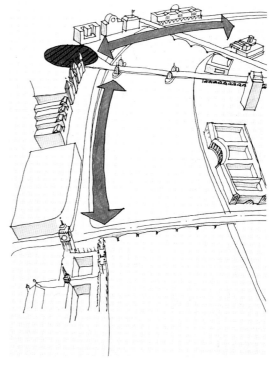

The final form of the building was a direct result of the critical nature of the site: for reasons of aesthetics and viability, the site demanded a large, distinct building that could take its place among the existing range of noble and robust River palaces.

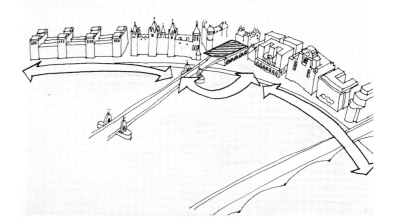

In a real sense Terry Farrell is a modern-day Vanbrugh. The parallel lies not only in the dramatic marshalling of extraordinary volumes of masonry, but in the wonderful effects concentrated on the skyline. It lies in a love of emphasis, of exaggeration. `I like repetition, even obsessive repetition,' he enthuses.

Robert Adam, who might at first seem the most unlikely admirer of Vanbrugh, was the first to recognize the particular quality of 'movement' in his architecture. In his famous *Essay on Architecture* (1773) Adam wrote:

'Movement is meant to express the rise and the fall, the advance and the recess, with other diversity of form in the different parts of a building, so as to add greatly to the picturesque of the composition. For the rising and falling, advancing and receding, with the convexity and concavity and other forms of the great parts, have the same effect in architecture that hill and dale, foreground and distance, swelling and sinking, have in landscape; That is, they serve to produce an agreeable and diversified contour, that groups and contrasts like a picture, and creates a variety of light and shade, which gives great spirit, beauty and effect to the composition.'

Here are precisely the qualities that epitomize Farrell's design for Charing Cross – 'rising and falling', 'advancing and receding', 'convexity', 'light and shade' and above all 'spirit'.

English baroque was all but assassinated in its moment of crowning glory by the imposition of Lord Burlington's rule of taste: even Wren was dismissed from the Surveyorship of the Kings Works. Here it has found a spiritual heir.

At Charing Cross Greycoat and Farrell have created architecture with all the presence, and dignity of a public building designed to be seen and enjoyed as a focal point in the townscape.

The press is regularly filled with laments that London lacks any equivalent to Paris's *grands projets*. What Charing Cross shows is that commerce, the private sector, is also capable of producing spectacular, eyecatching landmarks that can have enormous and immediate public appeal.

2

The air rights concept

Left: **The roof profile was always considered to be one of the most critical elements of the design, and numerous forms were studied at the sketch design stage. The final barrel vault roof saw a return to the traditional and simplest form for the covering of a railway terminal.**

Top right: **The grid of nine pairs of columns was set out from the centre spans of the existing brick barrel vaults below the railway tracks.**

Bottom right: **The position of the lift and service core resulted from placing it in the wide western platform at Charing Cross, originally laid out as a cab road through the station.**

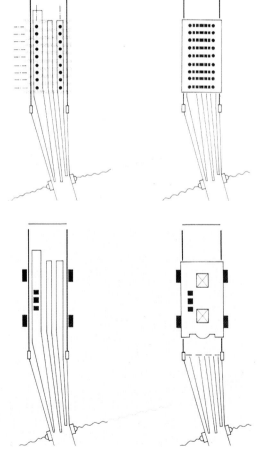

The idea of constructing an 'air rights' building over Charing Cross Station was born of two circumstances. First, Greycoat had taken over in 1985 a long-established property company, Law Land, dating from the late nineteenth century. The company owned a section of the former Buckingham estate, between Buckingham Street and Villiers Street. These streets stood on the site of the Duke of Buckingham's house: hence the original names George Street, Villiers Street, Duke Street, Of Alley (alas renamed York Place by a highway official who failed to notice the pun) and Buckingham Street.

Law Land's property on the station side of Villiers Street gave Greycoat a direct introduction to the site. And this was the time when Greycoat was constructing Victoria Plaza over the tracks at Victoria Station. The essential working relation with British Rail was already in place – with the Property Board, the operational management and the railway engineers.

Geoffrey Wilson, Chairman of Greycoat, explains: 'We recognized we were in a situation where we could act as catalyst. At Victoria Station we were also working very closely with Westminster City Council, not only the planners, but the highway department, and we sensed an opportunity to achieve major planning gains for the Council as well as for British Rail'.

It was clear to all that the environs of the station were badly run down. The properties in Villiers Street were decayed. The street itself was a rat-run through to the Strand. The station forecourt still suffered from the loss of E.M. Barry's magnificent cast-iron railings. Equally drab was the area underneath Embankment Place Bridge. Yet here was a place used by tens of thousands of people every day – a survey showed 3,000 people an hour crowded along Villiers Street.

Greycoat brought the three freeholders together: themselves, British Rail as owners of the station and Westminster as proprietors of the roads and Embankment Gardens. Part of the attraction to Greycoat was the magnitude of the problem. 'If a place is in desperate need of improvement', explains Geoffrey Wilson, 'you are far more likely to obtain the support you need. If you are seeking to build in a place which people like as it is, you are bound to run into stiff opposition.' And offices, of course, are potentially the most controversial of all developments. But here Greycoat themselves were to be the key to improvements of demonstrable public benefit.

To facilitate progress Greycoat entered an exclusivity arrangement with British Rail. Ronald Spinney, the Greycoat managing director who ran the project explains: 'A list of two categories of works were drawn up. For Westminster Council the potential environmental gains were these: the improvement of the entrance to Embankment Gardens from Villiers Street; the provision of a new bandstand for the popular lunchtime concerts; the creation of a water basin on the original line of the Thames, in front of Inigo Jones' York Water Gate; and the reordering of Villiers Street to give higher priority to pedestrians over traffic.'

For British Rail the list began with improvements to the station forecourt on the Strand, the reintroduction of the railings and the cleaning of Eleanor Cross (a replacement of the original designed by E.M. Barry). Building over the station also opened the way to improvements on the platforms themselves. Most significant of all was the creation of a direct continuation of the pedestrian walk along Hungerford Bridge into the station and on to the Strand. As it was, everyone crossing Hungerford Bridge had to descend stairs down to the Embankment and then climb up Villiers Street to the Strand.

Greycoat was determined to pursue a mutually advantageous scheme in a non-adversarial fashion. Their team consisted of Terry

The neglected state of the York Water Gate and the station forecourt were but two aspects of environmental deterioration in the surrounding area. For Westminster Council and British Rail (Greycoat's land-owning partners in the project), the scheme offered an opportunity to upgrade these peripheral settings.

Above: **Villiers Street. Although carrying up to 3,000 pedestrians per hour, the street was exceedingly drab, a prime candidate for improvements which included giving pedestrians priority over vehicles.**

Right: **Embankment Place, 1986. The layout of the site meant that the two most obvious entrances, Embankment Place and the Strand, were not available for an imposing entrance.**

Farrell and Company as architects, Ove Arup as engineers and an important but discreet role in the early stages for the Rolfe Judd Partnership, as planning consultants.

For Greycoat the essential decision, in Geoffrey Wilson's words, was 'where to invest the persona of the building'. The Strand frontage, the obvious prime site, was entirely taken up by E.M. Barry's Charing Cross Hotel. By contrast on the riverfront there was a distinct gap. The original vaulted roof of the train-shed had collapsed on December 5, 1905, while undergoing repairs, and had been replaced by a flat roof. In 1932 Harold Clunn in *The Face of London* had maintained the accident was 'a blessing in disguise, as it led to the disappearance of a hideous eyesore from the Thames Embankment'. Old photographs show, however, the arched train roof had a monumental quality, seen to advantage on the River, not unlike the great iron and glass roof of the Grand Palais on the Seine in Paris.

From a development point of view the potential lay in the substantial area of office space that could be created in the heart of Westminster, close to Trafalgar Square and Whitehall. Each floor that could be constructed above the tracks was potentially an acre in size.

The problem was access: not only the introduction of lifts and stairs between platforms, but the provision of a sufficiently imposing entrance, such as any tenant conscious of the rent he was paying was sure to demand.

One possibility was to create an entrance in Embankment Place itself, but this would have been right under the railway bridge. The south-west corner was already occupied by the recently restored Playhouse Theatre, while Carrara House on the other side of the railway bridge was the one part of the site Greycoat did not own.

Terry Farrell, therefore, determined to provide the new entrance halfway up Villiers Street. But the persona of the building was invested firmly and triumphantly in the new façade the air rights building creates, overlooking the River. Here it can best be seen, above the tracks on the Embankment. And by turning the building around like this to face the River it recalls the original riverside arrangement of Hungerford House and Market – a front door on the Strand *and* a front door on the River.

'We were always looking for a building of exceptional character,' Geoffrey Wilson explains. 'This is a very important site. Architecture of quality certainly costs more but it is money well spent. We wanted a building of drama,' he concludes emphatically. 'And it is. A proscenium arch.'

The Victorian trainshed, which collapsed in 1905, was of an appropriately noble scale, like other monumental iron and glass structures of the nineteenth century.

Charing Cross
station caters
for 120,000
passengers per
day – nearly three
times the density
of other London
terminals – and
the project
demanded non-
interruption of
the railway
operation during
construction.

Below: Aerial view
of the station,
c.1980.

The platforms at Charing Cross handle 120,000 passengers a day, a density nearly three times that of any other London terminus. Any proposal to build above them had, therefore, to fulfil two essential criteria. First, it had to make minimal intrusion on the platforms, and none at all on the tracks. Second, construction had to be programmed in such a way that not a single arrival or departure was delayed. More than this, British Rail retained the option of halting construction altogether should some emergency require it.

Charing Cross Station, like St Pancras (and Old Broad Street Station) is built up on a series of transverse railway arches that bring the trains in at the level of the Strand. As the land falls away to the river the arches become progressively taller.

Although the original construction of the arches was extremely sturdy, trains have become heavier over the years and the original timber platforms replaced in concrete. So it was out of the question to try and place further loads on them. The same was true of the flanking walls of the station.

Farrell and Arup therefore adopted a scheme whereby the new office block was entirely supported on columns sunk through the platforms and anchored deep in the London clay beneath.

The first crucial task was to place the columns so disruption to the station would be minimised. Dummy columns were set in place to see whether they would significantly impede the crowds of passengers arriving at rush hour. The tests showed no serious impediment would be created and the scheme was developed in detail.

Old records revealed a ramped cab road that had risen from the old stables in the vaults to platform level (long since filled in) which could also provide the route for the lift shafts. Service cores, with emergency staircases and firemen's lifts, were sited outside the station envelope, like giant buttresses, bypassing the platforms.

There were financial advantages in developing a design with a smaller number of large columns, as the most expensive element lies in sinking the piles for the columns. The system was therefore designed with two rows of nine columns that support a series of bow-string trusses from which the office floors are suspended.

The columns had to be sunk to a great depth to ensure their stability, and here the problem was that the shafts had to be excavated in the space beneath the vaults. There was no headroom for normal piling machinery, and the excavations were carried out by miners working with clay spades. Caissons were sunk through the wet gravel into the London clay, which is impermeable – 'like digging out very hard plasticine,' say Arup.

The piles were constructed with bell-bottoms to give the firmest footing, then carried up in reinforced concrete to basement level. Thereafter the columns are in steel. Where floors abut the columns, rubber bearings are used to ensure no vibration can be felt.

At the top the trusses take the form of a continuous arch tensioned by a 'bowstring' at the level of the top floor. A-frames, portal frames, vierendeels and mast and guy solutions were also examined but the bow-string trusses maximised the usable office space and respected the rights to light of adjacent properties. Better still the arches exactly mirrored the familiar outline of a terminus roof, giving the new structure instant acceptability in visual terms.

Often the form of a roof is dictated by the need to accommodate plant, but at Embankment Place most of the necessary equipment could be sited in the old railway vaults, allowing maximum advantage to be taken of the superb views at the top levels for offices.

The arches are of massive construction, rising a full two storeys. They consist of steel box sections two metres deep by one metre wide at the crown, and one metre square at the springing points. Each arch weighs sixty tons and was built with traditional falsework or centering.

The office floors are suspended not from the columns, but from a series of 'hangers' that descend from the arches. However, the office floors project beyond the main columns and, therefore, cannot be supported from the bow-string arches at this point. So a separate triangulated transfer structure, in the shape of giant coathangers one storey high, was devised that would sit on the main columns and cantilever out beyond them.

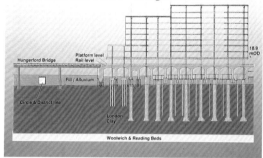

Embankment Place - Longitudinal section

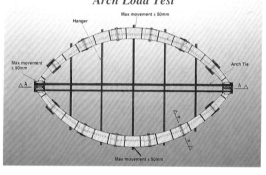

Arch Load Test

Top left: Longitudinal section of the foundations, showing the positioning of the columns in relation to the existing brick vaults.

Below left: The elegant form of the bow-string arches belies their massive construction. These carry the entire load of the office floors, and consist of steel box sections 2m deep by 1m wide. In this view, two arches are being load tested against one another at the works.

Right: Working above an operational train station meant that major works affecting the track and platforms levels could only be carried out between midnight and 4:00 a.m.

Obviously one of the most delicate problems was the removal and replacing of the original roof.

During the initial critical phase, the first level of the new building was constructed over the tracks to provide a clear working platform from which the rest of the structure could be erected. Work could only be carried out when the station was closed, between midnight and four o'clock in the morning. To ensure speedy delivery of material a lease was taken on an old siding at Hither Green in South East London and all materials were brought in by train at night. The wagons had their own cranes for unloading. During these precious hours the electric railway lines were switched off to allow work at track level.

To ensure maximum operational flexibility in the future British Rail had insisted that the new construction was wholly independent of the station below. In extreme circumstances the station could be rebuilt or even removed while people continued to work in the offices above.

Right: **Aerial view of project, 1990.**

3

The building design

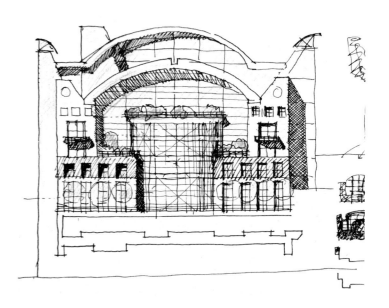

Left: **The evolution of the final form of the River facade, from concept sketches to final elevation.**

Previous page: **Completion of the last structural arch**

River facade of working model

The speculative office block has become the most notorious of modern building types, despised almost as much as the council-house tower block for the damage it has done to the fabric and skyline of our cities.

Terry Farrell firmly believes that commercial opportunities can be turned to public advantage and that the developer can be a better client than the company constructing its own prestige headquarters. 'The discipline is good. The corporate owner-occupier can all too easily become self indulgent, and lack the financial imperative to think hard enough to make the right decisions. The commercial developer, on the other hand, has far more interest in the spaces between and adjoining the buildings as they contribute significantly to the overall quality of the area which the developer has invested in. Such interest is also more long term with the developer, as the value of the properties for periodical rental reviews etc. is enhanced by the improved surroundings.

'I think the private sector has built some of the best pieces of urbanism anywhere – Bedford Square, Bloomsbury, all of these areas were built up by people having to make a mixture that worked commercially as well as environmentally'.

His brief at Charing Cross was the usual one of producing large areas of flexible floor space. At the outset, Geoffrey Wilson explains, there was still a demand for large areas of trading floor space, but it soon became evident that Big Bang did not, in practice, require anything like what was envisaged. Nonetheless it is for this reason that the floor-to-ceiling heights on the first and second floors are higher than those above.

For office space Greycoat have a standard general brief that is issued in advance to all their architects. This specifies floor loadings, ceiling heights and maximum distances away from windows. It lays down maximum lift waiting times and a general floor space ratio of one person to every 110 square feet (though less, of course, for the trading floor).

One of Terry Farrell's first moves on any site is to commission historical research. Even now the building is designed and completed he talks with intense enthusiasm and interest about the history of the site and its impact on the present. For him the organic growth of a city is a source of fascination, its history constantly shaping and guiding its future.

London is a city where the art of the possible had usually taken precedent over the ideal. Wren learnt this when his grand plan for rebuilding the city after the Great Fire was set aside by city merchants in a hurry to rebuild and unwilling to wait for streets to be aligned.

For the same reason numerous plans for replacing Hungerford Railway Bridge have never led to anything for the simple reason that, like it or loathe it, the bridge constitutes one of the vital transport links of the capital. Anyone looking at a map of London might expect to find a major road bridge at this point, leading from the South Bank straight to the heart of the West End, to Trafalgar Square, Piccadilly and Regent Street.

A powerful attempt to create such a thoroughfare was made in the 1870s when Northumberland House, the finest and grandest aristocratic palace in London, was destroyed (to the glee of the improvers) to make way for Northumberland Avenue. Not even its fabulous Jacobean frontispiece was preserved. But the promised bridge did not materialize.

A further proposal to remove Charing Cross Station to the South Bank and to replace the rail crossing with a road bridge was introduced about 1911. Prominent in the road lobby were architects such as Aston Webb and Reginald Blomfield. Nothing happened, but the scheme was revived in 1925 as a means of

Sections through the site, 1669-1833

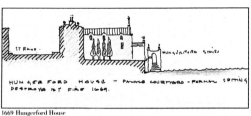
1669 Hungerford House

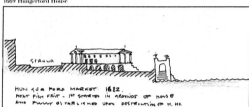
1682 Hungerford Market

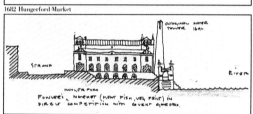
1833 Fowler's Hungerford Market

Sections through the site, 1845-1863.

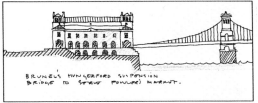

1845 Brunel's Hungerford Suspension Bridge

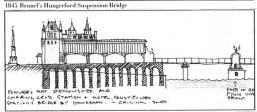

1860 Charing Cross Station and Hotel

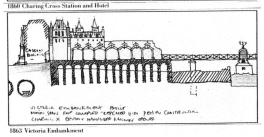

1863 Victoria Embankment

reducing traffic on Rennie's fine Waterloo Bridge, which showed signs of collapse.

A Royal Commission in 1926 recommended that Charing Cross Station be rebuilt on the north bank of the River, to the east of Buckingham Street. A new double-decker road and rail bridge was proposed, but the plan was rejected as a result of strong opposition from Westminster, Lambeth, the Royal Fine Art Commission and the Royal Institute of British Architects. The idea of a road crossing next re-emerged as part of Patrick Abercrombie's misguided post-war plan to remove all rail terminals from central London.

Most recently the demolition of Hungerford Bridge has been ardently proposed by Richard Rogers. He suggests the railways should stop on the south side and passengers be bulleted across the river in a suspended capsule. His proposals, illustrated in a breathtaking model at the Royal Academy, also propose that the Embankment be closed to traffic and rebuilt with steps down to the River. The essential problem with all such schemes is that Hungerford Bridge – both the railway line and the pedestrian walkway – has become such an established and well-used link that it is inconceivable it can be removed.

History provides the explanation. The name Hungerford Bridge comes from Hungerford Market, established under a 1678 Act of Parliament at the instigation of Sir Edward Hungerford, last impecunious occupant of Hungerford House. The house by this time was deemed 'so old and ruinous' it could not be rebuilt 'without great expense'. At the same time the York Buildings Waterworks were constructed to supply domestic water to the houses being created on the Buckingham estate.

The market, opened in 1682, was by the early nineteenth century in a very run-down state. It was in one of the adjacent riverside warehouses that Dickens was employed, in 1824 as a child of twelve, in a shoe-blacking warehouse (an archetypal 'sweatshop') at Hungerford Stairs.

By the 1820s Hungerford Market was condemned as 'little better than a monster dust-heap, and a cemetery for dead dogs and cats'. By Act of Parliament in 1830 a new Hungerford Market

Company took over and Charles Fowler, architect of the colonnaded market in Covent Garden, was commissioned to design a new market which opened in July 1833. The buildings consisted of a great hall, with surrounding galleries, smaller halls and an arcade. For all its handsome architecture the market did not flourish and in 1836, partly to attract custom from the south side of the river, Brunel was commissioned to design a suspension foot bridge across the Thames. This was not begun until 1841 and opened on 1 May 1845. In 1851 a lecture hall was added, but for all the efforts at improvement the market was never a financial success and when the Charing Cross Railway Company offered to buy the site, for a terminus on the northern bank, the offer was accepted.

The new terminus, designed by the engineer John Hawkshaw, opened on 15 May 1864. Brunel's suspension bridge had been removed four years earlier, the chains fortuitously being taken over for the Clifton Suspension Bridge at Bristol. Though begun in 1836, work halted and was only recommenced in 1860 after Brunel's death.

At Charing Cross the new railway bridge made use of Brunel's original piers, supplemented by new ones of purely functional design. A footbridge was incorporated on the downstream side with a toll that continued till 1877. Ten years later the bridge was widened, but has remained virtually unaltered since.

Farrell's guiding principle in the design of an office block is to avoid a building with endless rows of identical windows. He seeks a strong architectural theme.

The earliest sketches show that the first elements to shape the composition were the service cores – the emergency stairs and firemen's lifts, which for safety reasons had to be provided outside the station envelope. Naturally these quickly emerged as towers, and the first design with four towers is referred to as the 'mosque design'.

The initial preoccupations were largely with achieving a rational floor plan. Terry Farrell says, 'the building was merely perceived as a box. Discussions with Westminster planners then led to stepped

Left: Hungerford Market after 1845. Brunel's suspension footbridge was an unsuccessful attempt to bring custom from the south side of the River to the failing market.

Below left: Plan for a road crossing, 1906. The roads lobby has long had its eye on Charing Cross, although the frequent attempts to replace the environmentally efficient rail crossing with a road bridge have always been successfully defeated.

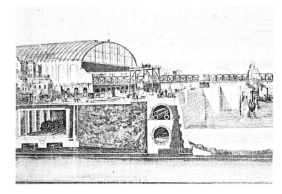

Bottom left: Cross-section of the Embankment at Charing Cross, 1863. By burying the underground railway (now the Circle Line), the sewerage and services beneath the new route, space was provided for new gardens along the boulevard.

boxes, six floors at the front, eight at the back, reducing the bulk of the building at the River end.' The idea of a tiered solution had already been explored in Farrell's earlier scheme for Vauxhall Cross.

Initially it was thought that the silhouette would be given interest by elements applied on top of the building, perhaps as plant rooms or as boardrooms, but as the arched roof emerged as the solution, it became the dominant element of the design. Ingeniously it allowed the insertion of an extra storey within the slope of the arch – providing seven and nine storeys above the station rather than six and eight.

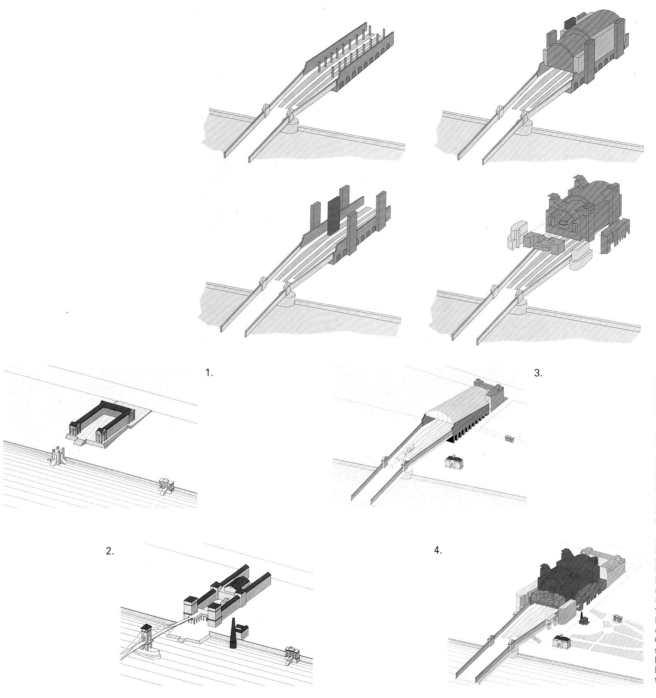

Far left: The existing structure and operational constraints dictated the basic layout and construction of the columns, and also severely constrained the positioning of the five main vertical cores. The four perimeter cores had to come to ground outside of the main station for reasons of fire strategy, while the central lift core was slotted into the wider western platform.

Left: The central structure springs from the nine bays of arches from which the floors are suspended, while the floors outside of the platform columns are of necessity cantilevered from the main structure. The final added elements bring the bulk down to the scale and character of the context.

Below: Turning the building around.
1. Hungerford Market 1682.
2. Hungerford Market and suspension bridge 1845.
3. Charing Cross station and Hotel 1865.
4. Embankment Place 1990. At each stage of the site's history, buildings have had both riverside and Strand entrances; the former, however, largely disappeared when Charing Cross station was built. Embankment Place has again turned the site around.

1.

2.

3.

4.

The final scheme
has established a
strong architectural
relationship with
the River, and takes
its place as a major
element in the
grand sequence of
riverside buildings.

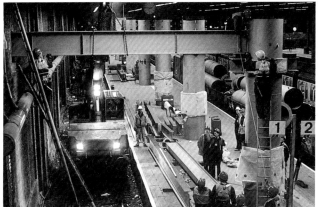

CONSTRUCTION

Far left: Excavating the bell-shaped bottom of the hand-dug piles.

Left: British Rail's operational requirements restricted construction activity on the platforms to the middle of the night.

Below left: The nature of the existing brick vaults below the station demanded that the columns be positioned at the crown of each vault.

Right: Erection of steelwork on the first level above the tracks. After this stage, construction could continue during normal working hours.

Left: Construction of the bow-string arches.

Right: Springing and construction of the arch, showing the supporting formwork.

Far left: View of knuckle joint and Macalloy tensioning bars.

Left: Construction of one of the lower bow-string arches.

Below, far left: Installation of a prefabricated cladding panel, all of which arrived complete with glazing.

Below, left: As construction proceeded at different rates, the lower front canopy building was clad while the main building steelwork was still being erected.

Construction sequence, showing progress at approximately 6-week intervals.

4

Farrell's Charing Cross

Left: View of completed air-rights building.

Evolution of the skyline from an air-rights block to a sculptured elevation.
1 & 2. The internal rationale of the building was worked out with the exterior perceived merely as a box. Discussions with Westminster planners led to stepped boxes, rising away from the Thames and reducing the bulk at the River end.
3 & 4. Initially, it was thought that an interesting skyline elevation would depend on elements applied to the top of the building, such as plant rooms or boardrooms. The use of an arch suspension structure, which emerged from discussions with Arup's structural team, allowed the skyline form to spring directly from the structural expression.
5. Finally, roof-top plant and conference suites on top of the service towers were added.

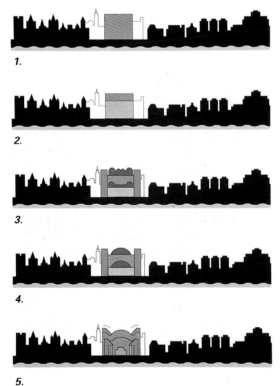

What makes the Charing Cross development so startling is the extent to which Terry Farrell has been able to marry two completely different building types – the arched steel roof of the railway terminus and the layered, repetitive floors of the modern office block.

From the River it has the look of a train-shed partly because the whole arch is darkened glass – just as the mouths of train-sheds, viewed from outside, always look dark, except at night when they are transformed by lights within.

Second, the arch is emphasized by the bold projecting lip over the glass front – well over fifteen feet in depth. Its wide underside positively glows in the beam of the floodlights – so much so that it seems to be internally box lit.

To achieve both the tone and the solidity he wanted, Farrell clad the major part of the building in a pale grey Sardinian granite, which from a distance harmonizes perfectly with the Portland stone of buildings on either side and across the River.

Both in colour and form the building has an immediately recognizable identity, even character. The towers, sloping down to meet the arch of the roof, have the look almost of insects' or crustaceans' legs, suggesting the building is tensed to move. The feeling is heightened by the remarkable decision to double-up the composition with a lower arched roof projecting – telescope fashion – from an upper one, and with the rear towers raised up above those towards the River. The sense of tension is also increased by the powerful chevron motif, consisting of aluminium tubes plunging down over the glass arch.

A chevron motif like this is what you might expect to find on a Thirties' car radiator. Farrell's use of it here is an instance of the daring way he uses motifs – on a vastly enlarged scale – to give a simple and unmistakable identity to a very large structure.

In the centre of the glass wall Farrell introduces a focal point in the form of a segmental bay, almost like the bridge of a ship. The curved glass he wanted would have been too expensive. Yet setting flat glass in a curving frame, he points out, creates the illusion it is bowed inwards – a scalloped effect like the fluting on a Doric column.

Internally it is a superb gesture, providing a 180-degree panorama of the River as soon as you step into it. Here again there is that sense of movement of which Robert Adam talked, of the rise and the fall, the advance and the withdrawal.

On the floor below, the third floor, you step out on to an extensive roof terrace that descends to a lower terrace immediately above the platforms, where the market stood over a century ago. This is the perfect venue for summer receptions. 'I was determined that the trains shouldn't just dive into the building,' says Farrell.

The feeling is not so much of garden terraces as of a succession of decks. Virtually all the cladding is metal, as well as the emphatic diagonally sloping railings, raked outwards like the streamlined prow of a speedboat. All this metal is dove grey in colour.

Originally Farrell had intended the walls of the terrace would be clad in stone, but when the tender came in the price was significantly above budget. The change to metal achieved the saving required and is actually an improvement. 'It's design on the run', says Farrell, 'and that's where the real skill lies.'

The detailing of the stair is particularly neat, worth a comparison with the kind of outdoor staircases you find at châteaux like Balleroi and Breçy by François Mansart. Two facing flights descend to a semi-circular half landing. The lower flight is an exact half circle divided into four. It appears to be a precipitous forty-five degree descent, but Farrell says this is an illusion from the cone shape. There is also a parallel with Borromini's extraordinary Sant'Ivo in

Rome where the exterior of the dome is treated like a staircase.

The colour so far is distinctly on the sober side, but Farrell provides a few brilliant accents in an almost luminous green. This is used on the bow of the River frontage and the tops of the four towers. The idea came from the weathered copper roofs on nearby buildings – the Festival Hall, Vincent Harris's Government Buildings, the Admiralty and the dormers on County Hall. Terry Farrell observes these greens range in tint from yellow to blue.

To achieve exactly the right mint green tone he hung test panels on the balconies of the Festival Hall across the River. And today, of course, it is no longer necessary to wait for the copper to weather – his panels arrive fully mature with a polyester powder-coated paint finish.

Geoffrey Wilson has aptly dubbed the tops of the towers 'Terry Farrell's eyebrows'. They were another example of 'design on the run' as the superb view they would command became apparent. The service shafts on the two riverfront towers were quickly replanned to provide a double-height executive suite that, now the building is complete, looks sure to be taken as the chairman's office. Once again Farrell introduces curved motifs with the panache of roof pavilions by Lutyens and Baker at New Delhi, a capped bow window with curved cantilever roof.

Farrell achieves a sense of modelling on his side elevations by a clever optical trick. The vertically linked windows are all sharply set back on the seventh floor – the top of the wall where the eye naturally focuses. 'This gives the feeling of solid walls, but the client doesn't loose the floor space on the floors below.'

Farrell takes particular satisfaction from the design of the roofs. They are at their most dramatic from the River end of the ninth floor, where from within the upper arch you look down on the lower one. 'I spent a lot of time looking at the roofs of St Pancras', says Farrell. Seen from the back of Scott's Midland Hotel the jet-black roofs assert themselves with enormous power, and Farrell has taken the dramatic motif of the gangway perched on the apex of the roof. Like St Pancras his arched roofs can give the impression of being elliptical in form, but in fact they are simply a segment of circle.

Detail of train-shed at St. Pancras station.

The robustness of Victorian train-sheds rests upon a stirring interaction between the glass and metal components of the roof. The distinctive linear lights are set against the black arched shed, creating an architectural language that is immediately recognisable.

Left: Core tower and executive conference suite.

The black of the roofs at Charing Cross does not derive from years of soot or pitch, but is laid in powder-coated aluminium sheets. In the aerial views the glass roofs of the two atriums can be clearly seen; these are constructed with vertical, but not horizontal, ridges so there is no possibility of water being trapped on the slopes.

One of the biggest challenges was to ensure the windows in the flanks of the roofs did not break up the elemental shape of the roofs. Another developer might have destroyed the effect by insisting the windows project as dormers, but here Farrell was able to recess the windows within the arch of the roof. The curved silhouette is maintained by continuing the girders (which would normally be on the inside of the roof) over the recessed windows.

These arched trusses – pierced with the kind of lozenge patterns found on nineteenth-century trusses, are seen at their most effective on the terrace outside the eighth floor. They also ensure that even there you do not see the serried rows of windows Terry Farrell so dislikes.

A tour of the roofs is a passport to the high-tech world you find on a Norman Foster or Nick Grimshaw building, with the same crisp elegance in all the metalwork detailing of floors and railings. Particularly striking are the free-standing, black spiral staircases.

Above: Detail of roof. The 'train-shed' origins of the roof design and detailing are readily apparent.

Left: Detail of River facade.

Right: View towards the River from 8th Floor suite.

Left: Bow window to River facade. Setting flat glass in a curving frame creates the illusion of curvature – a scalloped effect like the fluting on a Doric column.

Right: View from Waterloo Bridge. The curved silhouette is maintained by continuing the girders over the recessed windows.

5

Designing the interior

Above: **Entrance lobby, from Villiers Street. The three-storey volume of the entrance establishes the distinct presence of the larger air rights buildings within this otherwise modestly scaled street.**

In design terms Farrell faced the challenge that the building above the tracks would be perceived as almost completely separate from the streets below. The only practical place where the principal entrance could be sited was on Villiers Street. Once again Farrell shows himself a master of juggling with scale. Here is a three-storey triumphal arch that nonetheless manages to rest on dwarf columns.

It is a portico *in antis*, a *porte cochère* where the chairman and visitors can disembark out of the rain. But, so far from hiding the railway station above, Farrell has sought to highlight its drama. Two storeys away you look through a glass window to see the trains on platform one arriving and departing. Overhead is the suspended walkway that carries pedestrians from the Strand to Hungerford Bridge.

Within the recessed entrance the stonework can be appreciated at close quarters – banks of polished, dove grey Sardinian granite alternated with flamed textured Fountain Green, creating a striped effect.

As the main entrance is to some extent tucked away, Farrell had to ensure the entrance hall itself was especially memorable. There were, however, severe constraints. First, it had to be contrived within the system of brick arches under the station. This meant that the only source of natural light was from the entrance doors already recessed behind a portico. Second, the noise and vibration of the trains had to be eliminated, or reduced to a barely audible rumble. Given that the noise of an arriving train would normally be sufficient to halt any conversation, this was a formidable challenge.

Farrell's solution, with Arup's acoustic engineers, was to insert an arch within an arch, heavily insulated against vibrations. To give it style he changed the semi-circle of the barrel vaults into a segmental ceiling with a shallow arch emphasized by a projecting shelf concealing the lighting. Geoffrey Wilson says his fear was that it might look a little too 'like a tube station, but, as always with Terry, the scale ensures it does not'.

To gain enough space for an impressive entrance hall Farrell decided to link two vaults. The first is uncluttered, with a single dramatic focal point in the form of a spectacular fountain. Farrell is never hesitant about seeking inspiration from a whole range of historical sources – rather in the way a Renaissance or baroque architect would have looked freely to antiquity for motifs.

The fountain is inspired by Ledoux's perspective design of a house for the director of the Source of the River Loue. This takes the form of a huge cylinder or cotton reel, built across the mouth of a mountain torrent. Farrell takes the play with geometric shapes a stage further by resting the pipe on a rainbow arch, echoing the line of the vault. The bottom of the cylinder is levelled off to ensure the water pours out in an even stream. But while Ledoux's water spills out diagonally in a somewhat unconvincing arc, Farrell's runs perfectly smoothly -'like clingfilm,' he quips. But as it reaches the bottom it begins to fracture, creating an icicle-like display of prismatic reflections.

The sheer size and simplicity of the fountain diverts attention from the off-centre column (one of eighteen supporting the office building above). For a while Farrell played with the idea of placing the fountain off-centre too, but his decision is clearly the right one, as the fountain is to striking and powerful that you barely notice the column.

Farrell has a very subtle and original eye for mixing colours and here he creates a sense of luxuriance that evokes the rich marbles of Ancient Rome or Egypt. The richly veined, highly polished, Brazilian verde scuro on the walls looks like verde antico, while the pink speckled edging to the fountain recalls the red porphyry the Romans used for their baths.

Left: Rich and highly polished materials evoke the deep colours of antiquity, adding to the monumentality of the entrance lobby.

Right: Villiers Street frontage. The main office entrance deliberately appears as a monumentally scaled void in the street elevation.

The next challenge was to create an impressive link between the outer and inner halls, which meant breaking through the transverse supporting wall. A central column was essential to carry the weight of the vaults, and as always Farrell made a virtue of a problem: if there was to be a column it should be a column such as no other in London, and here inspiration came from the ultimate palace of subterranean architecture, the Moscow Underground.

At Kurskaya Station the vault of a circular vestibule appears supported by a capital so vast and tall that only the capital and the very top of the shaft shows above the floor. Farrell repeats the motif in simplified form and the spotlights set around the base cast shadows that suggest the fluting is actually scalloped.

Round the corner the high-backed banquet seats in more speckled pink terrazzo are grand enough for Cleopatra. The real sensation though are the extraordinary series of fountain pillars, designed with Peter Rawstone, that glimmer like luminous malachite. These consist of inch-thick sheets of pale green acryllic hung like suits in a wardrobe, with water trickling down the sides. But where the front edge is chipped away the lights trained up the panels refract with the brilliance of fibre optics. Here is an illusion with the cunning of a hologram.

The water trickles down into a basin set in a table made of the same terrazzo as the banquets. On either side are a pair of bronze table lamps, placed with the formality of eighteenth-century girandoles on either side of a pier glass.

The reception desk is also part of the architecture – giant, twenty-foot-long, bronze-tipped arrowhead.

The lift lobbies open off on either side of the reception desk. Inside the proportions give the satisfying impression of a perfect cube. They are panelled in two blond woods, American cherry inlaid with figured maple. In the corners vertical strips of mirror cleverly extend the space.

If you can, take the lift straight to the ninth floor. One of the major attractions of any new office block is usually the view. And from the top of the Charing Cross development you have one of the most spectacular and unexpected panoramas in the whole of London.

Go to the top of any of the towers in the city and you have a vista right across London. But you are usually so high that you might be in an aeroplane, and often you are looking down at an abysmal array of ugly roof extensions and air-conditioning plant. 'When I look at the rooftops of modern London all I see is a junkheap,' the architect Peter Foggo once vividly remarked.

The views from Charing Cross are instead more like those from the Pompidou Centre in Paris, fascinating because you are only just above the rooftops. The best views, of course, are those at the River end: downstream to St Paul's, upstream to County Hall and the Houses of Parliament. More unexpected is the view from the floor-to-ceiling picture window set in the lift lobby. This provides a stupendous sidelong view of the white stucco of Carlton House Terrace, right across St James' Park to Buckingham Palace.

At the Strand end the major landmarks are the spire of St Martin-in-the-Fields, the Globe of the Coliseum and the great, cream cube of the Royal Opera House.

In the foreground, it is true, is the dreary back elevation of Charing Cross Hotel, but Terry Farrell's experience on the Comyn Ching triangle in Covent Garden offers the solution. 'You clean down the brick, and then call in the brick stainer. He can stain each brick and hide all the ugly blotches and stains.'

On the top floor the arch of the roof expresses itself with remarkable power, the curve rising from five feet at the edges to a full fifteen in the centre. The lozenge-shaped windows at the ends are an attraction in themselves, as well as the view.

While no floor has quite as good all-round views as Level Nine, all the lower floors have particular qualities and features. On Level Eight, the lower arched roof rises more than halfway up the glass wall of the River end, giving a view rather like that from the cab windows of a steam engine. The flanks open out on to roof terraces, with the access doors set back behind the trusses, which have the look of flying buttresses over the aisles of a cathedral. Here too is one of the best views of the roofs, with their gangways and staircases, that invite one to explore. This is a world of its own where you could live, like the Sanpietrini, the masons who spend their lives on the roof of St Peter's, looking after the leads. From

Kurskaya metro station, Moscow. The entrance hall column motif, although simplified, was adopted directly from this masterful celebration of subterranean design.

Right: View towards the City from the executive conference suite.

Left: View of internal lightwell. Careful study of sunpath diagrams and the use of reflective glass for the upper levels have maximised the amount of light that reaches the lower office levels.

Right: View to the east from Level Eight terrace.

here the two service towers at the River end are seen to best effect, futuristic contraptions whose strange canopies suggest some ultra advanced communications system.

On Level Seven, the full extent of the space opens out with dramatic views across the River from the top of the outer arch. On either side are small patios with elegant free-standing spiral staircases providing access to the upper terrace. Here too is a gangway to the two-storey executive suites at the top of the service towers, with a conference room below and bow-fronted office above.

Level Six has small, sheltered roof terraces overlooking the River. Level Five has a balcony on the riverfront. On Level Four is the glass-fronted drum providing a 180-degree panorama of the River. Level Three has direct access to the large terraces over the railway lines. Here you look straight out to the fine belvedere tower of the Liberal Club and enjoy the view up the Thames to Westminster Bridge, which Monet painted in different lights. As the early morning mists rise, you see atmospheric effects as nowhere else in London from these riverfront windows. The clouds swirl in dramatic rolls, and the sudden glimpse of the sun, as a glowing red ball at eye level, is exactly what Turner would have painted. This is the kind of effect one expects at the top of the Jungfrau rather than in central London. On such days the constantly arriving trains complete a life-size tableau of canvases like *Rain, Steam and Speed*.

Levels Two and One are the largest of all, with extra floor space provided in the buildings along Villiers Street: here, however, you could never be bored, for trains are constantly moving beneath you. Particularly fascinating is the military precision with which the doors of a commuter train open at the exact moment the train halts, as the passengers rush to catch their connections.

Light is brought into the centre of the building by two atriums. Farrell made a careful study of sunpath diagrams and decided to clad the top levels in reflective glass to help bounce light down deep into the building.

Detail of rooftop access walkway.

Right: View of Level Seven office space. The vaulted ceiling intensifies the inherent drama of the view.

6

The urban context

Left: Station forecourt, early twentieth century. The definition of the forecourt was completely destroyed when the Victorian railings were removed after the war for road widening.

Below left: Interior of Charing Cross station, c.1865. The existence of the cab road – later altered to form a wide platform – allowed the insertion of lifts without disturbing any platform arrangements.

Right: Reinstated forecourt railings.

Below right: As no drawings existed of the railings, the design of the replacements was taken from archive photographs.

Simon Jenkins, when he wrote his weekly fusillade on London in the *Evening Standard*, once trained his sights on the forecourt of Charing Cross Station. Roundly lamenting the loss of the cast-iron railings along the Strand, he demanded the removal of the huge bale letters disfiguring Barry's opulent hotel front – 'as if we didn't know'.

The offending letters have now gone and to Terry Farrell fell the opportunity of reinstating the screen of stone piers, topped by globes and traditional cast-iron railings painted gloss black.

Farrell also secured control over the design of the platform area, though the concourse outside was handled by British Rail Architects in house. At Victoria Station the platforms below the new shopping centre are decidedly claustrophobic. At Charing Cross Farrell persuaded BR to allow him to create a feeling of space, counteracting the low ceiling-heights by opening up the station laterally. It was argued that the new vista across the platforms would never be appreciated as there would always be trains blocking the views, but Farrell won his way, and the feeling of spaciousness undoubtedly makes the platform areas more pleasant, particularly the much broader sense of light and air from the River end. Searching for the best precedent for a station with no natural lighting from above, his thoughts again turned to the Moscow underground, and commuters now enjoy platforms lit by glittering chandeliers.

George Millar in his classic Second-World-War escape story observed: 'The majority of main-line railways stations have stained and fouled their surroundings.' He was talking of Munich Hauptbahnhof, where he was hoping to smuggle himself on to a train to France and freedom, but what he says is alas true of most main-line termini in London.

Many major stations are surrounded by broad roads and swirling traffic – Euston, King's Cross, St Pancras and Victoria are all examples. Charing Cross too has the Strand at one end and Victoria Embankment at the other but the streets on either side retain their eighteenth-century character. The difference is that a particularly high proportion of passengers walk to and from the station, not just plunging straight down into the underground, but making a whole range of travel connections.

Those arriving by train emerge to catch buses in the Strand or to take the Northern and Bakerloo lines from the underground at Charing Cross. Alternatively they may walk down to Embankment Station to catch the Circle or District Line going east or west.

Tens of thousands of people also walk from the South Bank across Hungerford Bridge, not just to catch the Circle Line, but to walk up to the railway station, the Adelphi, the Strand, Covent Garden and Leicester Square. Many of those emerging from Embankment underground station into Villiers Street are simply walking through the station.

The Embankment is also the busiest single private bus stop in London, with numerous coaches bringing commuters to work in central London. Embankment, with four underground lines, is the perfect drop-off point. In addition river traffic makes increasing use of Charing Cross Pier, bringing people from Docklands and Greenwich.

The main roads were a given. Farrell's task was to improve the lesser streets flanking the station, Villiers Street and Craven Street as well as Craven Passage and Embankment Place, which run under it. As it was, these had deteriorated in exactly the way George Millar had observed, precipitated first probably by the sheer volume of dirt generated by steam engines, and a general reluctance of landowners and tenants to invest significant sums in

Left: Detail of the platform chandeliers.

Below left: The station was redesigned as a grand interior room with colonnades of the air rights columns at each side and a row of grand chandelier lights in the centre of the slightly arched ceiling.

Above: Playhouse Theatre from the Embankment, 1986. The music-hall theatre, built in 1906 and long used by the BBC, was restored at the same time as the Embankment Place development and returned to its original use.

Right: Villiers Street. Although not closed to traffic, careful surface design of this heavily-used pedestrian road discourages cars and allows the street to be 'claimed' by pedestrians.

property improvements.

The big difference, Farrell observes, between Charing Cross and the north London stations, was that it was predominantly a passenger station without a massive goods yard beside it. As a result both Villiers Street and Craven Street survived to a remarkable extent. Craven Street has the longest stretch of eighteenth-century houses in any of the streets south of the Strand. Numbers twenty-five to forty-five are all eighteenth-century and so are eleven to fifteen opposite.

A positive note had also been struck by the restoration of the Playhouse Theatre (designed by Detmar, Blow and Billeray, 1906) at the bottom of Craven Street.

Villiers Street had become a rat-run with cars, taxis and bikes using it as a short cut from the Embankment to the Strand, avoiding Trafalgar Square. Given the intense pedestrian use of the street – 3,000 people an hour – a potential hazard had developed. Westminster, therefore, placed 'no right turn ' signs at the end of Adam Street, where traffic emerged in the Strand, and when this proved ineffective introduced a positive barrier in the form of a traffic island. All these highway improvements are due for a review after a year of operation.

Villiers Street now works well as an example of what Farrell calls a 'pedestrian priority' street. Cars are not banned, but simply discouraged, and the introduction of paving instead of ashphalt prompts cars to drive more slowly.

Early on while stalking the site, Farrell noticed that pedestrians had disciplined themselves to walking on the left and broader sidewalks have been introduced, marked out by bollards. In a rare civic gesture, a substitute has been allowed for the usual hideous double yellow lines – in the form of yellow tiles set in the rain water gulleys.

When it came to designing the new frontages on the west of Villiers Street, Farrell was determined to maintain the scale and varied character of the façades opposite. The new elevations are clad alternately in a warm tan coloured brick and smooth uba tuba granite.

The planners were understandably concerned that black-looking granite might darken the street. But Farrell convinced them that very dark, shiny surfaces when they reflect light are actually brighter than matt red brick. 'Look at this bollard,' he says. 'Where the light catches the black gloss paint it looks white – just because of the reflections and the contrast.'

Railway arches have long attracted a remarkable range of uses and at Charing Cross both Greycoat and Farrell were determined that tradition should be maintained.

The best-known tenant was the Players' Theatre (not to be confused with the Playhouse Theatre at the bottom of Craven Street). This occupied two parallel arches under the station but was nearing the end of its lease.

This had its origin in Gatti's Music Hall. Carlo Gatti worked as a pastry cook in Hungerford Market and obtained a concession to sell coffee and ice-cream in 1856, and a music licence two years later. Soon after the station opened, Gatti's obtained a licence for music in the Arches. By 1875 'Gatti's in the arches' was listed among London's leading music-halls. The business – run by the family – continued to flourish after Gatti's death in 1878 and this was the music-hall that inspired Kipling's *Barrack Room Ballards*: Kipling had taken rooms in Villiers Street from 1890-91. In 1903 Gatti's closed but the arches were used at various periods as a cinema, until after the War it reopened as the Players Theatre in January 1946.

To ensure the theatre's survival Greycoat hired temporary premises during rebuilding. A new theatre, bar and restaurant has been provided and equipped, and the theatre been given a new long lease. The architectural design for the Players Theatre was carried out by Sandy Brown Associates under the leadership of David Binns.

The new theatre is three arches north of the old but in other respects identical. A model in a window beside the entrance in Craven Passage shows the layout.

The theatre is entirely contained in the length of one arch with steeply raked seating ensuring everyone has a good view. One of the concerns was that it should still be possible to hear the rumble

Left: Details of Villiers Street frontages, which relate to the scale of the east-side facades and recreate the environment of a true street. The highly-polished granite provides more ambient light to the street than is the case with lighter coloured – but non-reflective – materials such as brick.

The historic
Players' Theatre
was relocated in a
new theatre *(top)*
three arches to
the north of the
original, but in
other respects
recreates its
predecessor
(below).

of the trains above. By tradition an evening at the Players begins with a toast to the railway.

In the vaults nearer the River a weekend coin market had been established in recent years, selling a range of goods including military memorabilia. The vaults here now provide car-parking for the new offices, whilst the market makes use of them at weekends.

Craven Passage is not only the entrance to the Players Theatre, but a convenient link at low level between the Adelphi and Whitehall. To make it attractive and inviting Farrell has designed a row of small shops such as you might find in an arcade along one side. As in one of the arcades off Piccadilly all the shop fronts are built to a bold repeating design. This continues the tradition of small kiosk shops always popular around stations, but makes the arch much more stylish, without disguising the handsome brickwork. Riven York stone paving has been introduced to complement the brick, and this has the effect of making the shopfronts all the sleeker and more eyecatching. What makes Craven Passage particularly inviting are the large bold series of repeating lamps outside the shops, designed on the model of Chinese lanterns.

The space under the railway bridge was dark, dingy, cavernous and decidedly intimidating. Farrell's first move was to reduce the apparent width by inserting large columns, clad in smooth Brazilian uba tuba granite. At the same time the bridge above was refaced in stone. The introduction of the columns helped to give the pavements a distinct identity and once again Farrell has introduced shops, seeking to lend them the sense of the luxuriance found in an arcade, as with the new shops in Craven Passage. Once again the key is bold, emphatic lighting – this time in the form of enlarged versions of traditional globe street lamps.

7

Embankment Gardens

Far left: Embankment Gardens

Below: Embankment Gardens, c.1900.

Left: The York Water Gate in 1626 marked the line of the riverbank.

Right: The gate has been given a new water-based setting and landing stage.

Embankment Gardens, east of the building, were laid out after the construction of the Embankment in 1864-70 by Sir Joseph Bazelgette, the great engineer of the Board of Works. The original line of the River is marked by the York Water Gate, created in 1626.

In the seventeenth century the River offered the quickest and most convenient means of travel, and York House was the London residence of Charles I's favourite, the Duke of Buckingham. Though the house was demolished in the 1670s the York Water Gate has long been recognized as one of the milestones of Renaissance architecture in England. Recently it has been convincingly reattributed by John Harris to Inigo Jones, who points out that Jones could have seen De Brosse's designs for the arch in the Luxembourg Gardens (on which it is clearly modelled) while in Paris in 1614.

As part of the Charing Cross scheme a new water basin and fountain has been provided in front of the arch. During the excavations it was hoped that the original landing stage would be found, but as it was not, a new one has been constructed.

Greycoat have also provided Embankment Gardens with a new bandstand for the popular lunchtime concerts held here during the summer.

Old views of the Thames also showed the remarkable obelisk shaped tower of the York Water Works, which had operated on this site until the 1820s. As a garden ornament Farrell has reconstructed this, at third-scale, beside the Villiers Street entrance.

The marketing literature proclaims the Charing Cross development 'a new London landmark'. For once this is not mere hype. And it is never more true than at night when the riverfront positively glows in the floodlighting. This is an example of a very bold effect achieved with economic means: by training very white floodlights almost vertically up the façade, catching the overhanging arch and emphasizing the framing columns, the new building stands out as prominently as any on the riverfront. It also shows how much more attractive a white light is than the prevalent lurid sodium yellow. Smaller floodlights are also trained on the tops of the service towers, picking out the mint green bows and canopies above.

As a result Charing Cross is a focus of attention in the way large termini always were. John Pendleton in 1894 described one major English city station in these words: 'At night when the station approaches are illuminated with arc lights, and the ticket "sheds", refreshment rooms and bookstalls with incandescent lamps, it looks almost brilliant.'

One of the qualities of a great metropolis is that is continues to be awake and bustling until late in the evening, and by acting as a beacon to everyone driving or walking along the Embankment, or crossing the River, Terry Farrell's new Charing Cross building brightens the very heart of London.

Drawings

The realisation of Embankment Place involved the preparation of thousands of sketches, presentation, working and detail drawings. The following selection of presentation and scope drawings prepared by Terry Farrell & Company illustrate the main design features of the project.

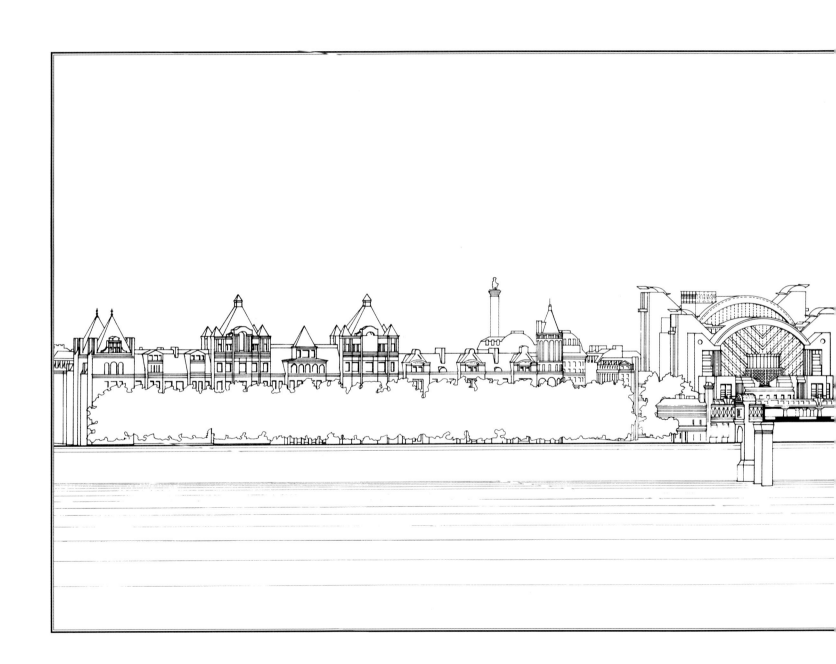

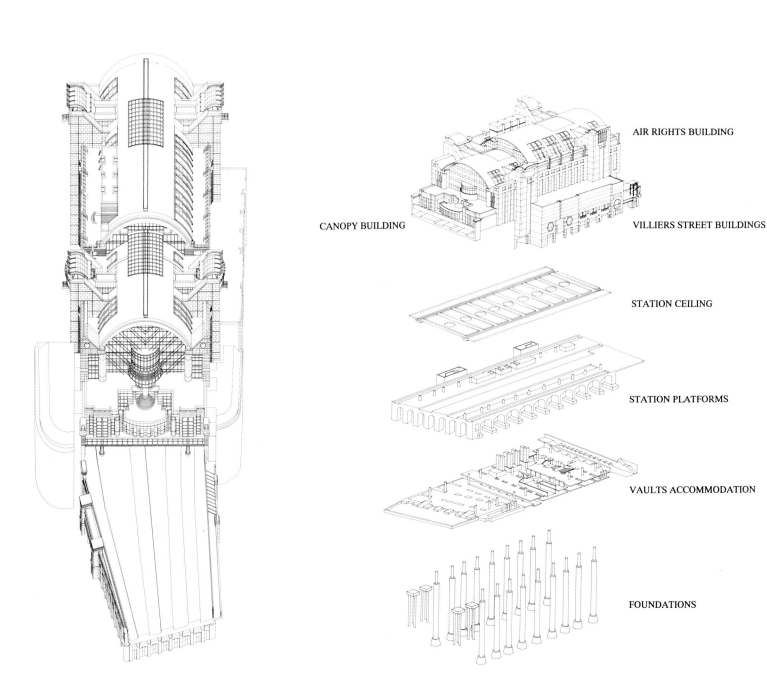

AIR RIGHTS BUILDING

CANOPY BUILDING

VILLIERS STREET BUILDINGS

STATION CEILING

STATION PLATFORMS

VAULTS ACCOMMODATION

FOUNDATIONS

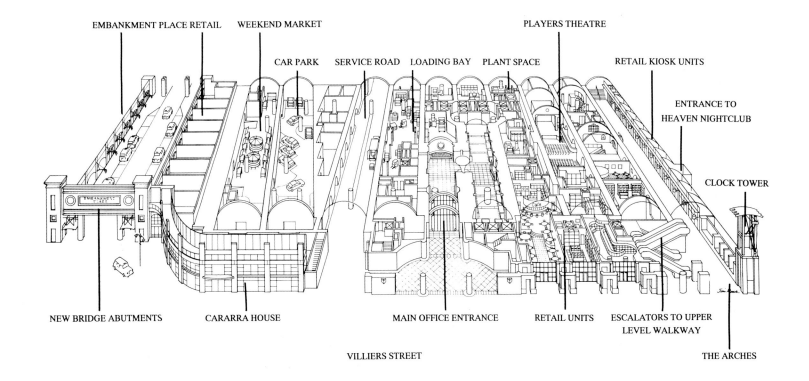

EMBANKMENT PLACE RETAIL

WEEKEND MARKET

PLAYERS THEATRE

CAR PARK

SERVICE ROAD

LOADING BAY

PLANT SPACE

RETAIL KIOSK UNITS

ENTRANCE TO
HEAVEN NIGHTCLUB

CLOCK TOWER

NEW BRIDGE ABUTMENTS

CARARRA HOUSE

MAIN OFFICE ENTRANCE

RETAIL UNITS

ESCALATORS TO UPPER
LEVEL WALKWAY

THE ARCHES

VILLIERS STREET

VAULTS ACCOMMODATION

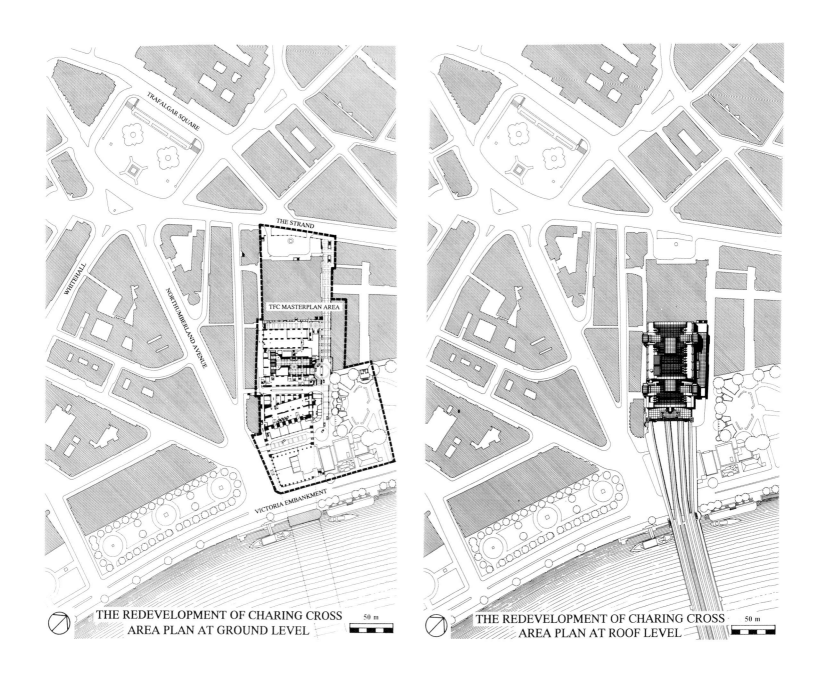

THE REDEVELOPMENT OF CHARING CROSS
AREA PLAN AT GROUND LEVEL   50 m

THE REDEVELOPMENT OF CHARING CROSS
AREA PLAN AT ROOF LEVEL   50 m

TRAFALGAR SQUARE

WHITEHALL

NORTHUMBERLAND AVENUE

THE STRAND

TFC MASTERPLAN AREA

VICTORIA EMBANKMENT

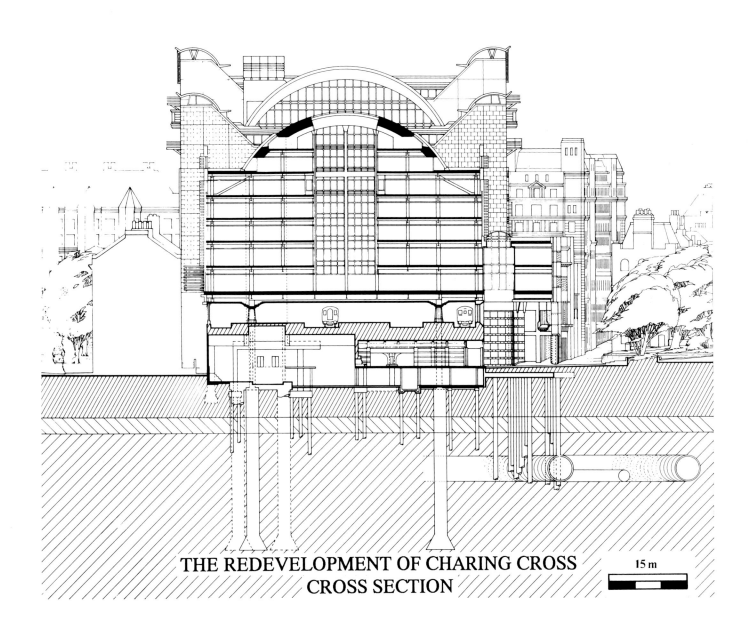

THE REDEVELOPMENT OF CHARING CROSS
CROSS SECTION

15 m

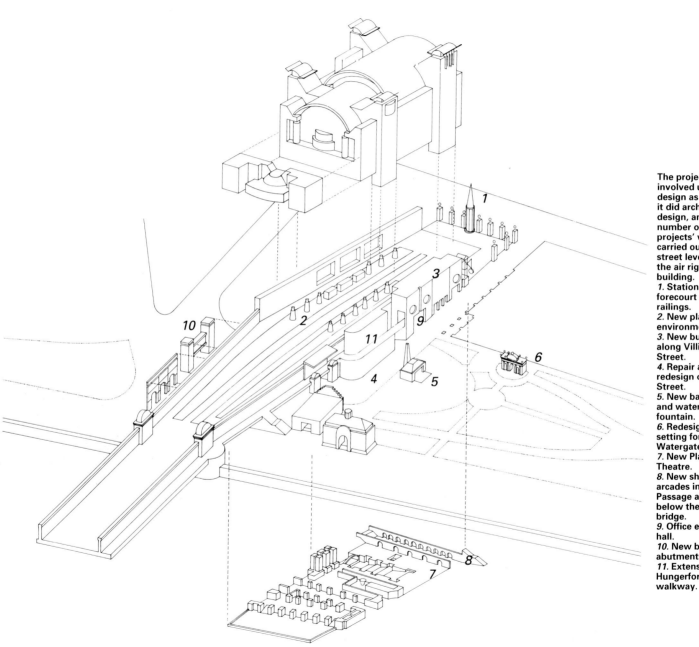

The project
involved urban
design as much as
it did architectural
design, and a
number of 'mini
projects' were
carried out at
street level, below
the air rights
building.
1. Station
forecourt and
railings.
2. New platform
environment.
3. New buildings
along Villiers
Street.
4. Repair and
redesign of Villiers
Street.
5. New bandstand
and water-tower
fountain.
6. Redesigned
setting for York
Watergate.
7. New Players'
Theatre.
8. New shopping
arcades in Craven
Passage and
below the rail
bridge.
9. Office entrance
hall.
10. New bridge
abutments.
11. Extension of
Hungerford Bridge
walkway.

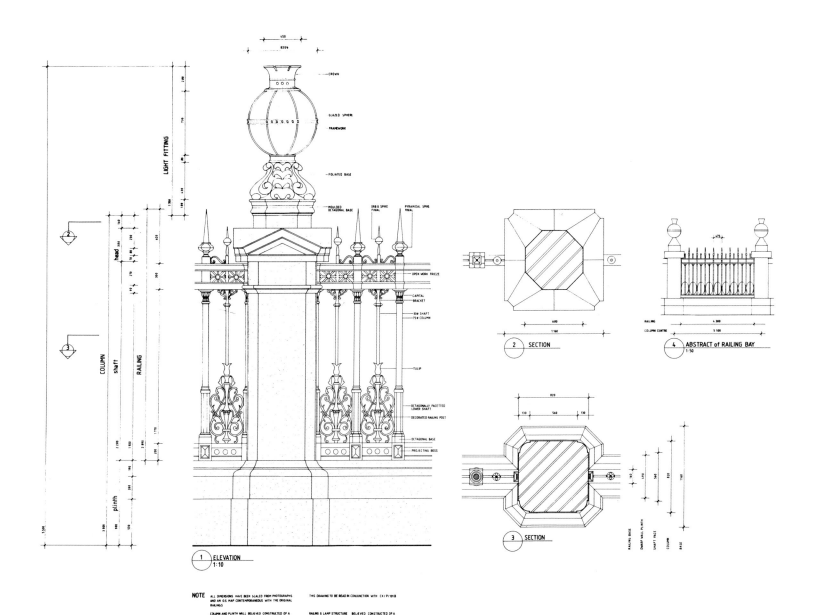

ELEVATION
1:10

SECTION

ABSTRACT of RAILING BAY
1:50

SECTION

NOTE ALL DIMENSIONS HAVE BEEN SCALED FROM PHOTOGRAPHS
AND AN O.S. MAP CONTEMPORANEOUS WITH THE ORIGINAL
RAILINGS

COLUMN AND PLINTH WALL BELIEVED CONSTRUCTED OF A
COMBINATION OF STONE, ARTIFICIAL STONE AND RENDER

THIS DRAWING TO BE READ IN CONJUNCTION WITH CX/P/1011 B

RAILING & LAMP STRUCTURE BELIEVED CONSTRUCTED OF A
COMBINATION OF CAST AND WROUGHT IRON

**Platform
environment
cladding
components**

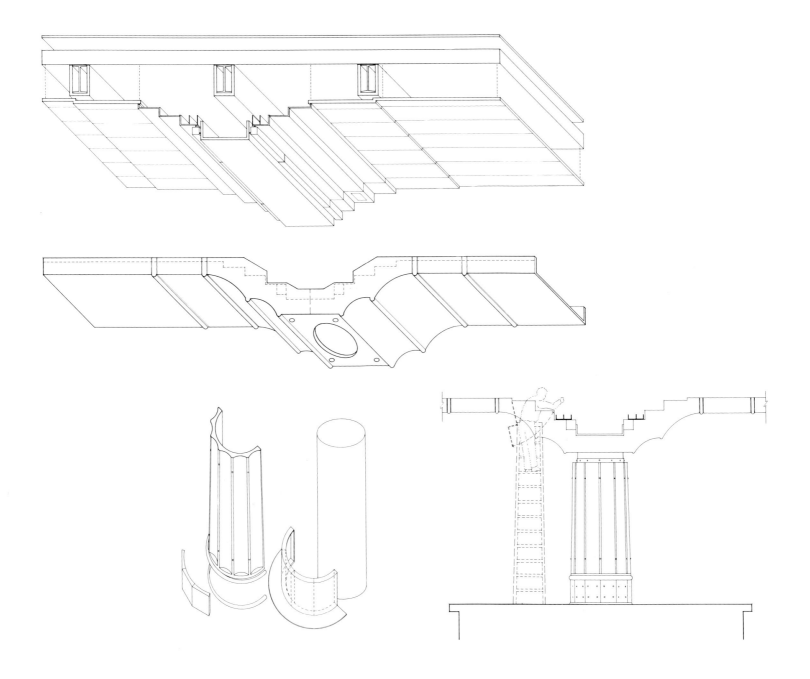

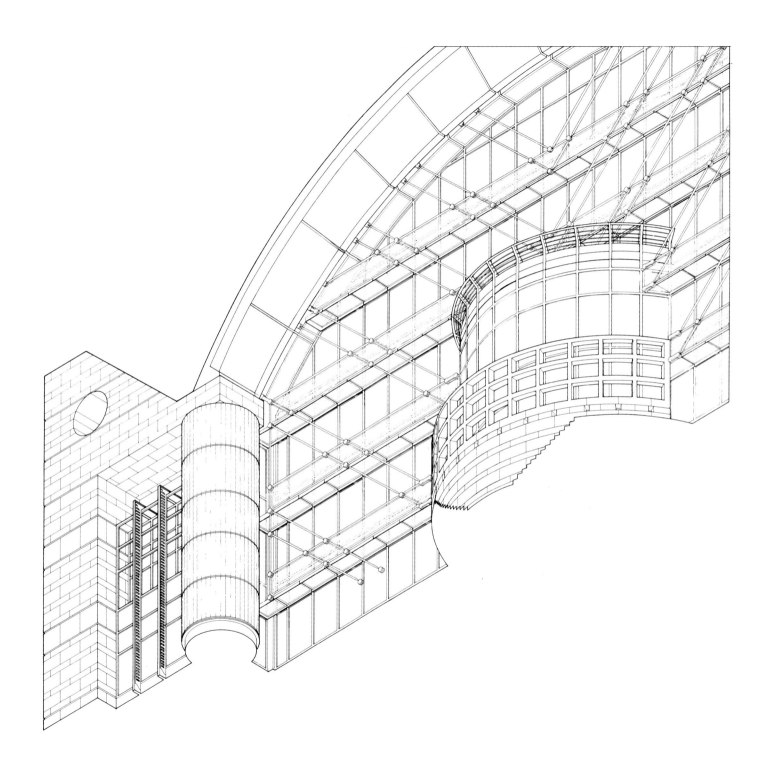

CHRONOLOGY

1985 January — Terry Farrell & Company approached by Greycoat Plc to undertake study of Charing Cross area and prepare design proposals for building above station.
May — Initial proposals brochure presented to Cllient.
August — Multi-roofed ('Mosque') design prepared.

1986 February — Arched form for Air Rights Building and Structure developed.
Preparation of Planning Application drawings and model.
March — Planning Application submitted.
May — Formal appointment of Terry Farrell & Company, Ove Arup & Partners and Gardiner & Theobald, Quantity Surveyors
June — Study models prepared.
August — Instruction to progress to Scheme Design.
November — Planning Approval granted (with conditions).
December — Project put on hold pending commercial considerations.

1987 March — Instruction to proceed to full detail design.
May — Villiers Street Buildings redesigned.
Conference suite design studies prepared for core tops.
June — Project proposals exhibited in 'Terry Farrell in the Context of London', Heinz Gallery.
Principal planning conditions approved.
Development Agreement signed with British Rail and Westminster City Council.
Appointment of Laing Management Limited and main contract signed.
July — Start on enablement works.
September — Players' Theatre closed.
Design of chevron bracing and core roof 'eyebrows'.
Preparation of final 'wood and brass' model.
Clearance of vaults begun on site.
October — Hungerford Bridge retail element introduced into project.
Villiers Street design model begun.
Hurricane of October 16th felled trees in Embankment Gardens.
November — Start on main construction works.
Station underpinning and hand-digging of piles begun.

1988 January — Form of Villiers Street buildings finalised.
First tubular steel column inserted through station platform.
March — Villiers Street ground slab started.
Last hand-dug pile completed.
Level 1 steelwork begun.
April — Concreting of Level 1 slab started
June — Level 1 steelwork completed.
Station roof removed.
August — Main steel framework started.
October — Villiers Street ground slab completed.

1989 January — Embankment Gardens improvements begun.
February — First cladding panel installed.
May — First arch started.
June — Steel erectors' strike.
July — Whole of office space let to Deloitte Haskins & Sells.
September — Embankment Gardens improvements completed.
October — Start of fitting out.
November — First toilet pod installed.
December — Escalators installed.
Last arch completed.
Concreting of slabs completed.

1990 January — Completion of forecourt improvements.
February — Stressing of arches completed.
Players' Theatre handed over.
April — Last cladding panel installed.
First performance in new Players' Theatre.
May — First concert in bandstand.
October — Practical Completion achieved, 2nd October 1990.
November — First rental tenant moves in.
December — External lighting adjustments tested on site.

1991 January — Installation of Villiers Street clocks.
April — Opening of upper level walkway.
June — External lighting completed.
September — Opening of refurbished cab shelter.

PROJECT TEAM

Client	Greycoat PLC	*Client's Letting Agents*	Baker Harris Saunders
Part Freeholders	British Railways Property Board	*Client's Letting Agents*	E A Shaw & Partners
Local Planning Authority	Westminster City Council	*Client's Letting Agents*	Hillier Parker May & Rowden
Architects	Terry Farrell & Company Ltd		
Structural and Services Engineers	Ove Arup & Partners	**Sub-contractors**	
Quantity Surveyors	Gardiner & Theobald	*Curtain Walling/Cladding*	Josef Gartner & Co
Services Quantity Surveyors	Mott Green & Wall	*Roof Cladding*	Hathaway
Management Contractor	Laing Management Ltd	*Atrium Roof Glazing*	Portal
Consultant Construction Advisers	Schal International	*Roof Glazing & Metalwork*	Hills of Shoeburyness
		Arch Cladding & Metalwork	The Wessex Guild
Landscape Architects	Cloustons	*Flat Roofs*	Prater Roofing Ltd
Assisting Cladding Consultant	Tibbalds Colbourne Karski Williams	*Primary Structural Steelwork*	Redpath Dorman Long
Player's Theatre Architect	Sandy Brown Associates	*Concrete Superstructure*	Diespeker Ltd
Space Planning Consultants	DEGW	*Secondary Steelwork*	Graham Welding
Assisting Planning Consultant	Rolfe Judd Group Practice	*Atrium Walls*	Tectonics
Specialist Lighting Design	Lighting Design Partnership	*Brickwork*	Vogue Developments
Services Advisers	Jaros Baum Bolles	*Hand Fixed Granite*	Conprodec/Stone Cladding Int.
Rights of Light Consultant	Michael Brooks & Associates	*Precast Cladding*	Dean Jesmond
Landscape Surveyors	Aworth Land Surveyors Ltd	*Drylining*	BDL Group plc
Client's Solicitors	Hamlin Slowe	*Suspended Ceilings*	SAS Ltd/Clarke & Fenn

Raised Floors	Tate Access Floors
Mechanical Installation	Rosser & Russell
Electrical Installation	Phoenix Electrical Co Ltd
Toilet Pods	Jordan Modular Building Systems
AHU Pods	Industrial Acoustics Co Ltd
Clock Tower & Roof	Cromwell Ironmasters Ltd
Clocks	Contarnex Ltd
External Soffits	Straeker Construction Ltd
Shopfronts & Glazed Canopies	Brent Metal
Entrance Hall	Davies Project Management
Specialist Acrylic Works	Talbot Designs Ltd
Vaults Lining	GM Building Systems Ltd
Station Windows	BSF Architectural Services Ltd
Movement Joints	Bestobell
Fire Protection	Morceau Aaronite
Additional Louvres	Greenwood Airvac
Joinery	Shapland & Petter
Platform Environment	R Mansell Ltd
General Metalwork	R Glazzard (Dudley) Ltd
Lifts & Escalators	Schlinder Lifts (UK) Ltd
Fire Shutters/Gates	Bostwick Doors
Refuse Equipment	Packawaste Ltd
Maintenance Equipment	Felco (UK) Ltd
Loggia Stone Paving	Grants
Gardens and Station Forecourt	Ardmore Construction Ltd
Cast Iron Railings	B Levy & Co
Facades to Hungerford Embankment	Bowmates
Bridge Abutments	Stone Developments Ltd
Repaving	O'Keefes/Cagneys
Substructure	Edmund Nuttall
Commissioning	Commtech
Building Management Systems	Honeywell
Sprinklers	Howe Fire Ltd
Stone Cleaning	Archer Stone
Brickwork Cleaning	Nigel Cox Ltd
Hand Dug Piles	J Murphy & Son

Architects project team and assistants

Stewart Abel	Frank Hickson
Titi Ajayi	Lizzie Hill
Keith Anderson	Mike Jarman
Chuck Barguirdjian	Mike Johnson
Alistair Barr	Mary Kelly
Steve Barton	Paul Langlois
Neil Bennett	Kevin Lewendon
David Beynon	Shane Lincoln
Toby Bridge	Paul Murphy
James Burrell	Ike Ogbue
John Campbell	Eileen O'Reilly
Helen Carroll	Maurice Orr
Francesca Carta	Richard Paine
John Chatwin	Louise Parker
David Chetwin	David Parken
Guy Cleverley	Dermot Patterson
Chris Colbourne	Terry Pawson
Andrew Cowan	David Quigley
Andrew Cowser	Claudine Railton
Christian Cuhls	Graham Sharpe
Andrew Culpeck	Ray Shiels
Susan Dawson	Mark Shirburne-Davies
Michael Doyle	Doug Streeter
James Edwards	Simon Sturgis
Tim Evans	Colin Taylor
Graham Fairley	Michael Taylor
Terry Farrell	Ashok Tendle
Carol Foster	Julian Tollast
Les Fuller	Tim Thompson
George Gardner	Eugene Uys
Christian Garnett	Vincent Westbrook
David Gausden	Duncan Whatmore
Vilma Gianini	Keith Williams
Steve Ibbotson	Ros Wilkinson
Maria Iwanicki	Chris Wood
Chris Hannan	Katie Woodruff
Jan Heynike	

Additional presentation material:

Sumati Ahuja	Chris Lane
Paul Bell	Mark Lloyd-Davies
Andrei Chelstow	Neil Southard
Ivan Green	Nigel Young